AF586777

promotes the detection of the criminal by a public and solemn transaction, under the management of the magistrates of the nearest city, associated with the priests, by putting numbers upon inquiry, and calling upon every one to clear himself, and warning all not to conceal the criminal.

The coroner in ancient times dealt chiefly with pleas of the Crown, that is to say, suits or proceedings in which the Crown was a party, as distinguished from suits between subject and subject. Hence the presiding officer derived his name, *coronarius* or *coronator*, e corona; and likewise its vulgar epithet "crowner," which, by the way, it first obtained in Scotland in the time of Edward I.

Though the powers of the coroner were much restricted by Magna Charta, he still retained considerable authority. The statute of Westminster, in the reign of Edward I., enacted, that none could hold the office under the degree of a knight; or none, at least, who had not lands in fee in the same county, equal to the yearly value of £20. This continued to be the case in Edward the Third's time; and in the fifth year of his reign, we find an instance of a man being removed from his office because he was merely a merchant. Accordingly, Blackstone complains that the coronership was, in his time, no longer undertaken by gentlemen of property; and though formerly no coroner would condescend to be paid for serving his country, yet for many years past they had only desired to be chosen for the sake of the perquisites. The practice, however, in this respect has greatly improved, and the coroners in our own time are in general persons of unquestionable respectability.

The *dignity* of the coroner is attested by the fact, that the Lord Chief Justice of the Court of Queen's Bench is, *virtute officii*, chief coroner of England, and has jurisdiction over all the kingdom; while the duties of the office are performed by humbler functionaries, who are coroners, each within his own particular district. Of these some are coroners *virtute cartæ sive commissionis*, within particular liberties,—*e.g.*, the Lord Mayor is coroner for the city of London.[1] There are also some ancient Franchises or Lordships in which the lord has, by virtue of a grant from the Crown, the power of appointing a coroner. The Cinque Ports, and the Dean and Chapter of Westminster, have each their own coroner. The Bishop of Ely

[1] 18th Edward IV.

nominates a coroner for the Isle of Ely.[1] The Master or Clerk of the Crown is coroner of the Queen's Bench, etc. etc.

The name occurs in a rhyming charter in Dugdale's *Monasticon Anglicanum*, granted by the Anglo-Saxon king, Athelstane, to the Monastery of St John of Beverly, A.D. 925, and containing the following lines:—

* * * * *

"If man be found slain, idrunkend,
Sterved, on sain John rike,
His aghen men withouten swike,
His aghen bailiffs make ye fight,
Non oyer *Coroner* have ye might.
Swa mikel freedom give I ye,
Swa hert may think or eghe see."[2]

That is, "If a man be found slain, or drowned, or dead, within the jurisdiction of St John's Monastery, and if his own (St John's) bailiffs find that the fight has been without foul play on the part of his own men, no other *coroner* may ye have. So great a privilege do I give you, as heart may think or eye may see."

There are also Admiralty coroners, who have jurisdiction in cases of deaths, and other matters belonging to a coroner, arising on the high seas. It is a curious instance of the jealousy of jurisdictions which existed in former times, that on the open shore, between high and low water mark, the jurisdiction of the Admiralty coroner and the county or district coroner alternated, the former acting when the tide was in, the latter when the tide was out. There are also coroners of the verge[3] of the palace, as well as a coroner of the Queen's household, who, in case of supposed murder or manslaughter within the precincts of the palace, take inquisition by a jury of 12 officers of the household. In the case of the valet of a Duke of Cumberland, the inquest was held by the coroner of the household; but, as suspicion fell upon the Duke, it was thought expedient not to have a jury of the household, lest such a jury should be thought by the

[1] Henry VII.

[2] The language of this charter is a mixture of Anglo-Saxon and English, *i.e.*, Anglo-Saxon in its transition state into English. The dialect in which it is written is that of the twelfth century, and must have been altered greatly from that in which it was originally expressed in the reign of Athelstane. The last line is equivalent in Anglo-Saxon deeds to the formula—"Be it known and seen of all men."

[3] 32 Henry VIII. ch. 10-7.

public to be influenced by their position—and a jury of the householders of the parish of St James' was summoned.[1]

With these exceptions, coroners, whether for counties, or districts, or boroughs, hold their office *virtute electionis*. The coroner of a county, or part of a county, is elected by all the freeholders of the county or district; the election is regulated by statute, and much resembles an election for a Member of Parliament. Coroners of boroughs are appointed by their respective Town Councils. A coroner's court is a close court for the purposes of the inquisition; and, acting judicially, he may exclude any one from the court who is there merely as a spectator or reporter, and not for the purpose of giving evidence.

The duty of coroner, in taking inquests, is defined and regulated by the statute, which enacts, that the coroner shall go, upon information of bailiffs, or other honest men of the county, to the place where any one is killed, or suddenly dead, or wounded, and shall forthwith command four, five, or six, out of the next township, to appear before him in such a place, and there to inquire, on their oaths, whether they know where the person was slain, whether it was in a house, field, bed, tavern, or company, and, if any, who were there? likewise it is to be inquired, who were, and in what manner, guilty, either of the act, or the force, and who were present, whether men, or women, and of what age they be, and if they can speak, or have discretion?

Besides holding inquests, *super visum corporis*, the coroner had likewise other duties to perform, now either obsolete or of rare occurrence, arising from being "*custos placitorum coronæ.*" He shall inquire concerning treasure found, concerning wrecks, and royal fish, as whales, or sturgeons. It is also the duty of the coroner to act for the sheriff, when just exception may be taken to that officer, from the fact of his being a party concerned, or from any other cause. The coroner also is conservator of the peace; he may cause felons and suspected persons to be apprehended; and may, of his own authority, stop an affray, and arrest parties breaking the peace.

The coroner, under this statute, also was to inquire, by means of those persons in the neighbourhood who were most likely to be

[1] Case reported in a London newspaper, charging the Duke with the *murder*. The Duke brought an action, and offered himself as a witness; he was subjected to a cross-examination, which completely cleared him of all suspicion of being the immediate cause of Sellis' death.

acquainted with the facts, concerning the death of any one slain; and these, being under the obligations of an oath, were to pronounce their verdict as to the cause of death, as well upon their own personal informations, as upon the evidence of witnesses who might be summoned and sworn to give evidence in the case. The statute further provides, that those who are found culpable by inquisitions in any of the manners aforesaid, shall be taken and delivered to the sheriff, and committed to gaol; and such as be found not to be culpable, shall be attached until the coming of the justices, and their names shall be written on the coroner's rolls. Then follow further regulations as to the proceedings of the coroner. If it happen that any man be slain in the fields or the woods, and be there found, it is first to be inquired whether he were there slain or not; and, if he were brought and laid there, they shall do as much as they can to follow their steps that brought the body thither, or of the horse which brought him, or cart, if perchance he were brought on a horse or cart? It shall be inquired also, if the dead person were known, or else a stranger, and where he lay the night before? And if there be any who are said to be guilty of the murder, the coroner shall immediately go into their house, and shall inquire what goods they have, and what corn they have in their grange; and if they be freemen, he shall inquire how much land they have, and what is the worth yearly, and further, what corn they have on the ground? He shall cause all the corn, and goods, and land, to be valued, as if they should be sold, and likewise, how much their freehold is worth yearly?

The coroner and jury shall then take a *view* of the body, and the wounds, and cuts, and other marks, if any have been strangled or burnt, or by other violence come to their death; and after the *view*, let the body be interred. But if the coroner find the body interred before a *view* be had, let him make enrollment, and take up the body; let it be openly *viewed* by the inquest, and then buried. In like manner, it is to be inquired of them that be drowned or suddenly dead, and after it be seen whether they be so drowned or slain, or strangled, by the sign of the cord tied strait about their necks, or about any of their members, or by any other hurt found upon their bodies; whereupon they shall proceed in manner aforesaid; and if they were not slain, then ought the coroner to attach the finders and all others in company. Also, all wounds are to be viewed, the length, breadth, and depth, and with what weapons, in what part the body is hurt, how many be culpable, how many wounds there be, and who gave the wounds, all which things must be enrolled in the roll of the coroner.

Then follow regulations regarding deodands, viz., inanimate objects, with which death has been caused, and which, according to the superstitions of the times, were to be devoted to the king's almoner, to be applied to pious uses, as "*res deo data.*" The king being, according to the quaint language of Sir E. Coke, "God's lieutenant on earth." Deodands, however, were abolished by the Act of 1846.

This statute is merely directory and affirmative of the common law of England; and although mention is made only of the death of persons slain, or drowned, or suddenly dead, yet the coroner ought to inquire of the death of all persons who die in prison, that the public may be satisfied that such persons come to their death by the course of nature, and not by duress of imprisonment, or by default of the jailor, whose duty it is to send for the coroner, in all cases of death, before the body is interred. Moreover, the words "suddenly dead," are not to be understood as meaning a dying suddenly of fever, apoplexy, or other visitation of God, but to relate only to death proceeding from violence or unnatural causes; and unless there be some reasonable ground of suspicion that the party came to his death by some violent or unnatural means, there is no necessity for the interference of the coroner. On several occasions they have been censured by the Court of the King's Bench for holding unnecessary inquests. Lord Ellenborough observed, that there are many instances of coroners having exercised their office in the most vexatious and oppressive manner, by obtruding themselves into private families, to their great annoyance and discomfort, which was highly illegal, and without any pretence of the deceased having died otherwise than a natural death. The coroner should, in general, wait until he is sent for by the peace officers of the place, to whom, it is the duty of those in whose house violent or unnatural deaths occur, to make immediate communication; yet, even recently, a case has been reported to me, of a coroner holding an inquest, although a satisfactory medical report as to the natural cause of death had been forwarded, in the hope of preventing the inquest.

The registration of deaths, in some measure, removes the practical difficulty which formerly existed, in determining whether an inquest should be holden or not, as it is the registrar's duty to ascertain and register the cause of death in all cases, and the duty of the coroner, to report to the registrar the finding of the jury. It is a matter indictable to bury a person that dies a violent death, before the coroner's inquest sat upon him.

As the inquiry of the coroner should be made while the body is fresh, and, if possible, while it remains in the same situation as when the death occurred, if he does not proceed forthwith, upon information of a violent or unnatural death (or even in cases of the natural death of a prisoner), to hold his inquest, he is liable to fine or imprisonment.

As to the length of time within which an inquest of death may be held, nothing definite has been laid down. In one case, the Court of King's Bench held seven months to be too late. And as such inquests must be held *super visum corporis*, the body should be in such a state, that information may be derived from an inspection of it. Both the coroner and the jury must view the body at the same time, for the inquisition proceeds on *view* of the body lying dead, and the oath ought regularly to be administered by the former to the latter *super visum corporis;* for, in truth, the body is part of the evidence before the jury, and, therefore, if they see it before, and not after they have sworn, a material part of the evidence is given when the jury are not upon oath.

From the necessity of this *view* of the body, it follows, that the coroner may order it to be disinterred within a reasonable time of the death, either for the purpose of an original inquisition, or for farther inquisition, if the first was insufficient.

If the body be not found, or have lain so long interred that no information can be obtained from the inspection of it; or if there be danger of infection by disinterring it, the inquest ought not to be taken by the coroner (unless he hath a special writ or commission for that purpose), but the Justices of the Peace, or other magistrates authorised to inquire of felonies, should take an inquest, on the testimony of witnesses. The coroner can only take an inquest on *view.*

According to the present method of proceeding at inquests, it is provided, by 6th and 7th Vict., chap. xii., that the inquest shall be held by the coroner only, within whose jurisdiction the *body shall be lying dead,* though the cause of death may not have arisen there.

Upon receiving notice of a violent death, or of one by casualty or misadventure, he issues his warrant to a peace-officer of the parish where the party lies dead, to summon a jury to assemble at a particular time and place, to inquire when, how, and by what means the deceased came to his death.

The modern practice is, to summon the jury only from the neighbourhood.

When the inquest is to be held upon a prisoner dying in gaol, the coroner issues his warrant to the jailor of the prison, requiring him to return twelve good and lawful men, prisoners within the walls of the prison, and, at a time specified in the warrant, to inquire into the cause of the death of such prisoner.

The court is opened by proclamation, and the coroner proceeds to call over the names of the jury. If a full jury be in attendance, they proceed, with the coroner, to *view* the body. They are then sworn in this form :—"You shall diligently inquire, and true presentment make, of all such matters and things as shall be here given you in charge, on behalf of our Sovereign Lady the Queen, touching the death of   , now lying dead, of whose body you shall have the view; you shall present no man for hatred, malice, or ill-will, nor spare any through fear, favour, or affection, but a true verdict give, according to the evidence, and the best of your skill and knowledge—so help me God."[1] The jury then view and examine the body, and the coroner should make such observations as its appearance naturally warrants; but it is not now necessary, as it was formerly, that the body should be before the jury and coroner during the whole of the evidence. The present practice is, to adjourn to another room, or to another place, where the coroner, having again called over their names, and ascertained that they are satisfied with the view, details briefly to them the object of their inquiry, viz., to ascertain by what means the deceased came to his death. Proclamation is then made by the officer for the attendance of witnesses; or where it is deemed proper to conduct the inquiry in secrecy, he calls in separately such as know anything concerning the death, and as each appears, the coroner takes down his name and place of abode, swears and examines him. After each witness has been examined, the coroner should inquire if the jury wish any farther questions to be put; and when the examination is closed, he should read over his deposition to the witness, and subscribe it along with him. The coroner may commit witnesses who may have been summoned, for contempt in not attending. In the absence of material witnesses, from whatever cause, it is in the discretion of the coroner to adjourn the inquest to a future day. When all the witnesses have

[1] Jervis on the office, etc., of Coroners, p. 390.

been examined, the coroner usually sums up the evidence to the jury, and explains the law, if it should appear to him necessary to do so. At any time during the investigation, it is the privilege of the jury to call back any witness for re-examination; and they are also entitled to the opinion of the coroner on any point of difficulty in law that may suggest itself to their minds.

As juries proceeded upon their own knowledge, as well as upon the testimony of witnesses, it was formerly held that they might from their own cognizance of the fact, have returned a verdict without any evidence being adduced before them; but, in later times, a different opinion has prevailed, and it is now agreed, that if a jury-man be acquainted with the facts of the case, he should be sworn as a witness, and give his evidence publicly to his fellows in court. But when the coroner is informed, that any person summoned as a juror has any evidence to give on the subject of the inquiry, it is the better course not to swear him on the jury. When the jury find it necessary to retire to consider their verdict, an officer must be sworn to attend them, and to keep them without meat, drink, or fire, until they are agreed. For this purpose the officer takes them to a room, where they are kept by themselves until they are unanimous, or till a majority, to the number of twelve, agree. When the jury have given their verdict, the coroner draws up the inquisition, to which both he and they set both their hands and seals; and when the verdict amounts to murder or manslaughter, the coroner grants a warrant for the committal of the person found guilty, for future trial, and binds over the witnesses to appear at the court where the trial is to take place. In these cases the coroner is obliged to take down the evidence in writing, after the inquiry has terminated, or before, if there be danger of infection.

If the jury return a verdict of *felo de se*, the body is not entitled to Christian burial, as we see in the Rubric, at the commencement of the Burial Service of the Church of England, which is confirmed by statute. In former times the body of a suicide was buried in the highway, with a stake driven through it. That barbarous custom has long been obsolete, and was formally abolished by statute, which directs that bodies of *felones de se* shall be privately buried in the churchyard.

The verdict of *felo de se* is very rare; and juries, for the most part, bring in a verdict of insanity where a party has died by his own hands. I have known a coroner make an apology to a medical man for returning a verdict of insanity, to secure Christian burial, in opposition to medical evidence. Hence, our great dramatist remarks,

1st Clown. Is *she* to be buried in Christian burial that wilfully seeks her own salvation?
2d Clown. I tell thee she is, therefore make her grave straight: The Crowner hath sat on her, and finds it Christian burial.
1st Clown. But is this law?
2d Clown. Ay, marry is't: *Crowner's quest law.*

—Hamlet.

The coroner issues his warrant for the burial of the body; and if the person was baptized, and not excommunicated, the clergyman is obliged to read the burial service of the Church of England, and may be cited into the ecclesiastical court in case of refusal. To those who are acquainted with the burial service, this may seem rather hard upon the clerical conscience.

It is now agreed that the coroner's inquest must in all cases bear evidence on oath,[1] as well for the party accused or suspected, as for the Queen, because the proceeding is not so much an accusation or an indictment, as an official inquiry into the manner in which the party came by his death. The Statute provides, that both in England and Ireland, whenever upon the summoning or holding of any coroner's inquest, it shall appear to the coroner that the deceased person was attended at his death or during his last illness by any legally qualified medical practitioner, it shall be lawful for the coroner to issue his order for the attendance of such practitioner, as a witness at such inquest, and if it appears to the coroner, that the deceased person was not attended at, or immediately before his death by any legally qualified medical practitioner, it shall be lawful for the coroner to issue such order for the attendance of any legally qualified medical practitioner, being at the time in actual practice, in or near the place where the death has happened, and it shall also be lawful for him to direct the performance of a *post mortem* examination, with or without any analysis of the contents of the stomach or intestines by the medical witnesses who may be summoned, provided that if any person shall state upon oath before the coroner, that in his or her belief the death was caused partly or entirely by the improper or negligent treatment of any medical practitioner, or other person, such person, etc., shall not be allowed to perform or

[1] Even a Peer in giving evidence cannot be examined "on his honour."

assist at the *post mortem* examination. And whenever it shall appear to the greater number of the jurymen, at any coroner's inquest, that the cause of death has not been satisfactorily explained by the evidence of the medical practitioners or other witness or witnesses, they are empowered to name to the coroner, in writing, any other legally qualified medical practitioner or practitioners, and to require the coroner to issue his order for the attendance of such practitioner, etc., as a witness, and for the performance of a *post mortem* examination, etc., by him, whether such an examination has been performed before or not; and if the coroner shall refuse to issue such order, he shall be guilty of a misdemeanour at common law. A fine of £5 is imposed on the medical practitioner for non-attendance; and the whole proceeding is closed by the result of the inquiry being recorded in what is technically called "the inquest," viz., a formal writing on parchment, embodying the verdict or finding of the jury.

We may well be surprised and astonished, that in England (enlightened England?), medical men were actually shut out of a court of inquiry into the cause of death, prior to the year 1836. Till then, there was no law providing for their attendance on such occasions, and the necessity of calling a medical man to give evidence, might have been questioned by the justices, and payment disallowed. The bill then passed "to provide for the attendance of medical witnesses at coroner's inquests,"[1] while enforcing attendance by a fine of L.5, leviable, if need be, by distress and sale of offender's goods, prohibits the medical witness from making a *post mortem* examination, unless the coroner see fit; thus reducing the evidence to a mere matter of opinion.

There is another act relative to the payment of fees to coroners, medical witnesses, etc., and other matters, which I need not mention in detail.

In proportion as the jury perfected itself as an instrument for the ultimate trial of guilt or innocence, it ceased to be applicable to preliminary investigation; and, there is scarcely an imperfection in the existing coroner's inquest, which may not be traced to the change which has taken place in the functions of the jury since its institution. In former times the judge and the coroner alike called together a certain number of persons from the neighbourhood in which a crime had been committed, selecting those who were most

[1] 6th and 7th Wm. IV., c. 89.

likely to be acquainted with the circumstances; and having administered an oath to them, *inquired* what they knew or had learned of the matter.

For the purpose of the coroner, this proceeding was, unquestionably, far better fitted than for those of the judge. An investigation thus made, could scarcely be exhaustive of the possible evidence in the case, though it was likely enough to furnish sufficient information to enable the coroner to select the proper parties, both for accusation and examination, and thus effectually to contribute towards what a Scotch Procurator-Fiscal would call "getting up the case for trial."

But, an alteration in the ideas which had hitherto prevailed regarding the functions of jurors, had gradually been working itself into practice, and was at last embodied in a statute, to the effect that the "jury ought not to see or take with them any other evidence than that which was offered in open court."[1] For judicial purposes, the improvement was incalculably great, and paved the way for that complete development to which the system afterwards attained.

When applied to the coroner's inquest, however, its operation was far from beneficial. It at once converted into a species of irregular and imperfect trial of guilt or innocence, what was originally, and what is still intended to be, a preliminary investigation into circumstances and occurrences, of which all that can be said in the first instance is, that they are unusual.

To the fact of its having thus become a species of bastard trial by jury, in the modern sense, we attribute the following leading defects of the coroner's inquest:—

1st, Its inefficiency, arising from the cumbersome nature of the proceedings, the delay and consequent opportunity afforded to criminals to escape, and to partial witnesses to make up a spurious case.

2d, Its inevitable publicity, of the fact of which (notwithstanding the power of closing his door which the coroner possesses), any one who looks into the *Times* newspaper, may convince himself.

3d, The expense which must attend it, however conducted, so long as the services of so many persons are required.

4th, Its odious character in the eyes of private families of respectability. And

5th, It seems passing strange that medical men should have so

[1] 11 Henry IV.

little to do with an inquiry into the cause of death, seeing that they are, beyond all others, competent to give opinions calculated to elicit the truth, and to guide a jury in forming an accurate judgment.

This has not escaped the graphic pen of the most graphic writer of our day, in exposing social abuses—Mr Dickens; see "Bleak House" for an example of a "crowner's quest."

"The office of a coroner," says Sir John Jervis, a recent writer on the subject, and now Lord Chief Justice of the Court of Common Pleas, "whether in consequence of the rust and relaxation inseparable from ancient institutions, or of the inefficiency of its officers, has fallen from its pristine dignity, into the hands of those who are, in some instances, incompetent to the discharge of even their present limited authority." And few circumstances can demonstrate its inefficiency so clearly as the numerous Acts of Parliament passed in recent times to amend or improve it.[1] The verdicts returned by coroners are sometimes most unscientific—often downright nonsense. Take a solitary example:—"Having taken cold on the 15th, and had given him sweet turnips, pigmeat, and herb-tea, gilt underground, ground ivy, chamomile-blossoms and honey, after violent vomiting and inflammation, in a state of exhaustion, died accordingly."[2]

Notwithstanding these and many other imperfections, however, the coroner's inquest possesses a thoroughly English character; it has a powerful effect on the public mind to suppress clandestine mischief in families actuated by avarice—is a check upon those having the charge of idiots, aged people, or illegitimate children, and exhibits a determination on the part of our fellow-countrymen, from the very outset of criminal proceedings, to give to the suspected party the refuge of an appeal to his peers, from the possible partiality of officials, and, at the same time, to secure the like protection to those who have suffered injury. It is a good, a useful, a necessary law, but probably the clumsiest and most complicated (*looking to the single object in view*) that the world has ever seen. Its jury is frequently composed of men utterly incompetent to perform their onerous and responsible duties. It is lauded by a few and condemned by many. It is a relic of a bygone age, and, as conducted, it is of little real value in practice.

[1] See Baker's Law of Coroner.

[2] Granville on "Sudden Death," p. 59, a work in which numerous "verdicts" !! of the most unscientific character, extracted from the Register, are given.

AUSTRIA.

In Austria, whatever room there may be for political improvement, the comfort and safety of the people are carefully attended to, and, accordingly, we find they possess a well-ordered system of inquiry into all cases of death taking place suddenly, or under doubtful circumstances.

In every town and district of country there are medical men officially appointed by Government; and by them, and other members of the medical profession of the highest grade, sworn in for the occasion by the magistrate, the inquiry is conducted.

It is the duty of these officials to investigate all cases of death by violence, by poisoning, by the improper use of remedies prescribed by apothecaries, deaths occurring under the hands of quacks, and even cases where a physician has been in attendance, if the relatives wish it. They must inquire into all cases of exposed or murdered infants, of procured abortions, and premature delivery. The cause of death, even where it is manifest, as in the case of a man shooting himself in the pit of a theatre, is sought for in the brain and other organs. Indeed, the entire inquest is made to hinge on medical evidence, and in every case a *post mortem* examination is required. The body is thus made to tell its own tale to a jury of competent persons, who, from their knowledge of pathological anatomy, are able to report to the civil authorities distinctly, what was the cause of death; and in cases of violent death, even to deduce from appearances of the body or traces of disease, whether the case was one of murder or of suicide. Thus farther inquiry is either satisfactorily stopped, or is set on foot in a regular form, and on a sure basis.

EAST INDIA POSSESSIONS.

In our Indian Possessions, the coroner's inquest is admirably conducted, and is certainly a great improvement on the English law.

The causes of all deaths occurring under suspicious or extraordinary circumstances, are carefully and minutely investigated.

At all stations beyond our frontier, and at military bazaar stations, courts of inquest are convened by the commanding officer, on the requisition of the officers in charge of the police.

At bazaar stations within the frontier, investigations are made by the nearest competent civil authority, or failing such, by the commanding officer.

Courts of inquest are composed of not fewer than three European officers, with a captain as president. *A medical officer is invariably to be detained, in order to examine the body and assist the court by his professional opinions*, and a series of very valuable suggestions is given for his guidance.

The court shall assemble as soon as possible, upon information of death under suspicious or extraordinary circumstances. The members shall proceed to view the body, and the place where it was found, and shall record an accurate description of all their proceedings. With regard to the body, the probable age, size, sex, make, peculiar marks, colour of body and hair, and all jewels, clothes, etc., etc., shall be described. All evidence which may either directly or indirectly throw light upon the cause of death, is to be carefully recorded, and a verdict to be returned in the usual form.

The whole proceedings of the court, composed of military officers, and held at stations where there is a deputy-judge advocate-general, are forwarded to him; and these, with his report thereon, are transmitted to the commanding officer, and by him again immediately forwarded to the adjutant-general of the army.

FRANCE, ETC.

In France, and, I believe, in Prussia and Bavaria, there are medical men officially appointed by Government in every arrondissement, to examine into the nature and cause of all injuries and sudden or suspicious deaths, etc., etc. In large towns these officers are sometimes numerous; for instance, in Paris, there are 7 physicians or surgeons, 3 accoucheurs, 3 physicians engaged in the treatment of mental diseases, and 8 chemists attached to the "tribunal of first instance."

Besides these the high court of appeal has 3 physicians, 1 surgeon and 1 chemist, as part of its staff.

When any injury, crime, or death, occurs under mysterious circumstances, the commissary of police repairs to the spot to make inquiry, and sends for the medical officer of the district, who investigates and reports to the procureur-impérial, who either goes or sends a deputy, to obtain additional information, and if there are reasons to believe the suspicions to be well-founded, he orders the medical officers to make a thorough professional investigation into all the circumstances bearing upon the injury inflicted, or if death has occurred, its nature, and how that event actually arose.

The reports thus made by these two public officers, are transmitted to the proper authorities, and legal proceedings are afterwards commenced before the usual criminal tribunal.[1]

SCOTLAND.

Few persons, probably, are aware that the office of coroner, now altogether unknown in Scotland, at one time existed in that country. In the ordinance of Edward I., "*super stabilitate terre Scocie*," he is specified as a necessary and subsisting officer, and he frequently makes his appearance in the oldest records of the Justice-Ayres. One principal part of his duty seems to have been, by arrestment of the person, effects, or otherwise, to secure the compearance of offenders for trial. In the record of the Justice-Ayres begun at Jedburgh 31st October 1502, there is an entry of the "*bona arrestata per Coronatores de Jedworth*," consisting of "oxin, ky, hors, scheipe, ruks of corne, nolt," and the like, belonging to a number of different persons there named. In the same book there is entered a precept under the hand of the king, dated 12th April 1504: "Our sovrane lord commands Maister Richard Lawson of ye Herigge, till tak sourete of William Dudyngston, *crownar* of Twedaile, under ye paine of doubilling of the unlaw of tene punde. That the said *Crownar* shall enter Jok Wilson's dwelland in the Glene upon Tueyd, in ye next Justice-Ayre of Peblis that sal be halding, sic lik as the said *Crownar* suld half enterit him, in the last ayre halding of before at Peblis."

There are several other entries in which the name of *crownar* or *coronar* occurs, where interesting details regarding the manner of what was anciently called "taking up dittay," in Scotland, will be found. To illustrate the practice of inquests in Scotland, I shall give a brief outline of the manner in which they are conducted in the county of Mid-Lothian.

[1] For the information relative to France, etc., I am indebted to the kindness of Dr Webster of Brook Street, London.

1*st.* In all cases of sudden death, the district constable repairs to the place where it has occurred, collects information, and sends off a report immediately to the superintendent; and, in cases of rape, child murder, or concealment of pregnancy, the *constable* is to ascertain, with precision, all appearances exhibited, such as marks of feet, blood, etc. etc. If there be any circumstance calculated to raise ground of suspicion as to the death, such as external marks of violence, bruises, fractures, etc., the constable is to apply to the nearest medical man without delay; and, after an examination, is to obtain a certificate, and forward it immediately to the superintendent. In all cases of serious assault, and where death is likely to occur, the constable, without delay, procures the assistance of the nearest medical man, and sends off a report, as before described; and instructions are given as to what circumstances the medical man is to certify. Upon receiving such a report, it is laid by the superintendent before the procurator-fiscal of the county, who either acts upon his own responsibility, or occasionally takes a fresh precognition, and prepares a case to submit to the crown-agent, to whom the police reports are also frequently sent, and whose instructions are thereafter acted upon.

Notwitstanding our national reputation for superior education, it does seem strange to me that our police constables should be considered competent to ferret out the necessary evidence in cases which must, from their very nature, be complicated and obscure, even to those whose daily business it is to investigate the matters involved in such inquiries. Under our active and zealous county superintendent, who is responsible for the reports, and who personally investigates all doubtful cases, this system is said, by lawyers, to work well enough.[1] They, however, can be no fit judges

[1] By a report of the superintendent of the county police, laid before the General Meeting of the County, and published in the newspapapers of the 18th July, I perceive that the duties required of that force might well exempt them from undertaking medico-legal investigations, even were they otherwise qualified for the duty. The force consists of 21 men, who have under their surveillance, as it were, a county of about 397 square miles, with a population of nearly 60,000. It is their duty in criminal cases, to investigate all offences coming under their notice, report thereon, cite witnesses and others, to attend trials (which frequently occupies them from 10 to 2, 3, and 4 o'clock) and discharge the duty in summary cases, amounting to well-nigh 500 annually. As a road police, they enforce the provisions of the General Turnpike Act, and obtain convictions amounting to between six and seven hundred annually. They discharge the

in such matters. Fancy, for a moment, a constable's report quashing a will case! And is the cause of a man's death more easily discovered than a testator's intentions? Is the punishment or the prevention of crime of less importance to the community, than whether Jack left to Tom or to Bill L.100?

2*d*. But this initiatory step has not the sanction of a legal enactment. It is, in fact, an order to the district constable by the superintendent, and I admit it to be an important one, in so far as that by it cases of sudden death are now brought under the notice of the legal authorities. That is one step in advance.

3*d*. There is no fund to remunerate medical men for the trouble and responsibility thus put upon them, and I am not aware that they ever receive any remuneration.

4*th*. Procurators-fiscal of counties, etc., were formerly paid by fees, exacted in each individual case; and an inducement was thus held out to investigate every one. In some counties, to such an extent was this practice carried, that fees to the amount of L.2000 per annum were known to have been claimed. Now, however, the practice is changed; those functionaries are paid by fixed salaries, and I am doubtful if the same zeal will be displayed in bringing up cases for trial.

Another apparent step in advance, is an enactment in the new registration bill, where, in cases of new-born children exposed, or found dead, or in cases of persons found dead, a report is to be sent to the procurator-fiscal, who, "in case of a precognition," is to report to the registrar before he can enter the case in the register. I may here remark, however, that the birth and burial of still-born children are not to be registered, and thus every facility is afforded for concealment of pregnancy, and for the crime of child-murder. The procurator-fiscal does not appear to be bound by the act to investigate the "cause of death," and hence the entries in the register in such cases are worthless. For example:—In a case of an illegitimate child, some months old, found dead in bed, which came recently under my own observation, and was reported

duties appertaining to all statutory offences. They have districts allotted to them as a patrolling police both for night and day; and as a check upon them, they visit householders at certain points, from whom they may hear complaints and receive signatures, which are transmitted weekly to head quarters, the average number of visits thus paid by each per annum amounts to 664.

to the procurator-fiscal, no *post mortem* examination took place. It was the second child by the same mother found in similar circumstances within two years, and both were supposed to be *mislaid*, although the coroner of Middlesex, in a population of between eight and nine hundred thousand, reports that not one in 200 children found dead in bed, has lost its life in consequence of being *mislaid*.[1] The case mentioned stands in the register, "found dead in bed." Again, a man was taken suddenly ill in a canal boat, and died in a few minutes. The case was reported to the procurator-fiscal, no *post mortem* examination took place, and in the register the cause of death is entered as "unknown."

That we do want a court of inquiry to ascertain the cause of all sudden and suspicious deaths, few will be bold enough to deny. In some counties, I doubt not, examinations are made with care; in others, I unhesitatingly assert, that there is frequently no inquiry at all, or one conducted more for form's sake, than with the view of ascertaining the cause of death. Several medico-legal cases have been reported to me, where the legal authorities showed either an utter indifference in the performance of their duty, or at all events a remarkable tardiness in fulfilling it; and where, in consequence, the medical men, either to satisfy their own natural anxiety, or that of the relatives, as to the cause of death, *at the last hour* performed a *post mortem* examination, without receiving legal authority. They were immediately censured or severely reprimanded, while the fault originated with the lawyers.

Prior to the establishment of our rural police—and some counties still have no police—there was no one to report cases of suspicious deaths in country districts; and, within my own knowledge, every now and then cases occurred in which an examination ought to have been sanctioned, and possibly would have been ordered, but for the parsimony of the exchequer, which refused to pay fees for medical reports or *post mortem* examinations, and hence sheriffs refused to grant warrants for such examinations. I believe that to be a prominent cause of the apparent laxity on the part of the legal authorities. Take two or three examples:—The dead body of a man, respectably dressed, was found in a plantation. I reported the case to the procurator-fiscal, and he requested me to give my opinion as to the cause of death. I refused to give it without receiving permission

[1] See "Lancet."

to make a *post mortem* examination. That was not granted; no means were taken by advertisement or otherwise, to ascertain who the man was; and the body was buried—"unknown." A man was found dead at the side of a hedge, with an empty phial, which had contained laudanum, in his pocket; he was presumed to have poisoned himself, and was buried without examination. An active parochial inspector requested me to examine the body of a man found dead in a ditch on the roadside. I refused to comply without an order from the proper authorities; it was not granted, on the ground that the *constable* did not think there was any suspicion of foul play," and the body was ordered to be buried, as in the two former cases, "unknown." Yet it was known that this man had been drinking with two companions—that they all left the dramshop tipsy, but in apparent health—and that the body mentioned was found dead a few hours thereafter.

There is a small parish on the east coast of Scotland, containing scarcely 2000 inhabitants. Within the space of five years, the bodies of 14 persons, who had died from unknown causes were brought to the churchyard for interment. Some were found on the beach, having been in the water for various periods of time. The names of some were discovered—others were unknown. One was actually buried as the wife of a certain gentleman, though the body of the said lady turned up alive thereafter! The cause of death was always taken for granted; no examination was ever made, nor even, I believe, thought of. In one instance it was known that the body found was that of one of two men who had been on board a vessel off the coast, but how he had been drowned remains a mystery. Three of the bodies were found in plantations; and in each of these cases suicide was assumed to be the cause of death. Why that conclusion was arrived at, no one can tell, except that, in one instance, the body was suspended by the neck. Of the other two, one was found alive on the roadside, apparently not well, while shortly before he had been seen quite well in the neighbouring toll-house. He was put into a barn, found dead in the morning, and buried without farther inquiry. Thus, in five years, in one small locality, 14 bodies are buried, and the cause of death in all, is unascertained!

Take one other example, and one too, which loudly calls for a remedy to be provided for the defective state of the law:—A married lady, during the absence of her husband, gave birth to a dead child, which could not be the offspring of her husband. Public report alleged the medical attendant of the family to be her paramour, and the servants of the establishment made no secret of the more than suspicious intercourse they had witnessed. The husband returned, and, in order, as was supposed, to obtain decisive evidence of his wife's guilt, he continued to occupy the same house, though he never slept with her. Meanwhile the medical man continued to attend the lady, and resided very much in the house, and people did not hesitate to predict that, if the lady should again become pregnant, her husband's life would not be a long one. After many months, the husband took suddenly ill and died, exhibiting all the symptoms of having been poisoned. The indignation of the whole district was roused; hand-bills were stuck up in all public places, charging the adulteress and her paramour with the murder of the deceased, and calling on the legal authorities to investigate the case. A neighbouring magistrate sent one of those hand-bills to the procurator-fiscal of the county, with a letter urging him to have a *post mortem* examination, and to investigate the cause of death. That functionary replied that he was aware of the reports that were abroad, but that he did not consider himself bound to investigate the matter, unless he was asked to do so by the nearest relatives of the deceased[1] (these being the lady! her father, and brother). No investigation took place. Immediately after the funeral the lady announced that she was pregnant, and in due time was delivered of a child. She continued to live in the mansion-house till she produced another child, confessedly to the medical attendant, who finally deserted his own wife and family, and removed with the widow to a distant part of Scotland, where they lived together till a few years ago, when he died.

The crime of concealment of pregnancy, leading as it too frequently does, to that of child-murder, is far more frequent than is generally believed, and, in comparison to the frequency of the crime, is seldom punished. Indeed, amongst the lower orders it is hardly regarded as a crime at all; and even in the higher ranks there are but too many who do not scruple to use means to get rid of the conception, when illegitimately pregnant. In March 1853, a regular establishment was detected in London for the systematic destruction

[1] I have known the same reply given by others in very suspicious circumstances.

of infant life, under the name of "premature confinement," which never terminated successfully for the child.[1]

In December 1844, Mrs H. called for me, to say, that her neighbour, Mrs D., who had been a widow for two years, had lately been pregnant, and that, as she now appeared to have been delivered, and as the child was not forthcoming, child-murder was strongly suspected. I had good reason to believe the report to be well-founded, and communicated the case to the procurator-fiscal. He gave me a warrant to examine the woman, and report to him. I found all the usual appearances of a woman recently delivered: the mammæ were filled with milk, the belly was loose and pendulous, the uterus large, with the os open and dilateable, and there was an abundant lochial discharge. She strenuously denied having been pregnant, and I committed her to the custody of the constable, for the night. She sent for me in the evening, to say that she now thought she must have been pregnant, and must have miscarried at a very early period, as "no formation was visible." She was sent to prison in Edinburgh, and I reported that she had been recently delivered of a child. A few days thereafter I was informed that, after the time of the presumed birth, Mrs D. had been seen with a large parcel at the house of the reputed father, and that he had borrowed a spade from one of his neighbours, on the same evening. Acting upon such information, I sent the constable to him to demand where the child was buried. The man was thrown completely of his guard, thinking Mrs D. had told all, and he conducted the constable to the spot, where a full-grown child was disinterred. Dr Traill and I were appointed to make a *post mortem* examination, when we found the following appearances:—The mouth and nostrils were occluded by a thick piece of cotton cloth, firmly bound over the face, and secured by bandages tied tightly round the neck, so as to produce a blackish and congested mark under the knots. On the front of the trachea there was an ecchymosed spot; the umbilical cord had been divided with a sharp instrument, but not tied. After a minute and careful examination of the body, we certified that the child had been born alive, and at the full period, and of course reported all the particular appearances, etc., etc. In this case every link of evidence was taken with the greatest care, and a chain of proof obtained apparently amply sufficient (at least to a mind un-

[1] Granville on "Sudden Death," p. 183.

accustomed to the intricacies of legal lore) to convict for concealment of pregnancy, if not for the more serious crime of child-murder. The woman was not even brought to trial, and on her return home confessed her guilt to her neighbours.

A lady overheard a discussion amongst her female servants as to whether it is better to have a natural child in the town or in the country. The case was deliberately argued, and they came to the conclusion that a child was more easily disposed of in towns. It is melancholy to contemplate such a state of society, and to know that no attempt is made to apply an effective check.

But, leaving the legal, and turning to the medical profession, a very unpleasant duty devolves upon me, from the discharge of which I would gladly refrain. It is painful to reveal the shortcomings of some unguarded, if not unworthy, brethren; but the interests of truth and morality compel me to speak out. Many practitioners are able to recal some instance of apparent disregard of human life on the part of others, or such malpractices as should demand investigation; and the profession could well spare those who would shrink from a searching and effective inquiry into the cause of death in any case. Examples of professional delinquency are happily of very rare occurrence, and, as a body, we may well be proud of the high principle and honourable character of its members. I have already recorded one case where a medical man was implicated, and will content myself by relating another, equally attended with most culpable circumstances. A lady was pregnant several months before her marriage. To conceal the fact, and for other reasons, she secured the services of a medical practitioner from a considerable distance. At her confinement, under the influence of chloroform, an unusually large quantity was used, and no one was present with the medical man, save the lady's husband. After the birth of the child, the medical man left his patient, who never rallied. She died in a short time, whether from flooding or from the effect of chloroform is unknown. The child, unwashed and undressed, was carried off by the medical man to a distance of 15 miles. There it was given out to nurse, and died in a few hours. No effective inquiry was ever made, and the relatives of the lady did not even know that she had given birth to a child, until after her funeral!

I cannot resist adducing one other case, in which both the legal and the medical men were outwitted:—A new-born child, wrapped up in an apron, was found in a well, where it had lain for several days. The clergyman of the parish and the parochial inspector, on their own responsibility, ordered a surgeon to examine the body. The procurator-fiscal thereafter ordered another practitioner to re-examine and report, and a certificate was given that the child was born alive. Public rumour fixed upon a girl in a neighbouring village, as the mother, and she was given to understand that she must go to the procurator-fiscal to be examined. She brought a younger sister from a distance of 36 miles, and presented herself to the legal authorities sooner than had been anticipated, anxious, as she said, to have her character cleared without loss of time. A medical man, who was altogether unacquainted with the girl (not he who examined the child), was desired by the authorities to examine her and report. The culprit cleverly persuaded her younger sister to submit to the examination—she was examined accordingly, and certified to be a virgin!

It is always more easy to find fault than to suggest a remedy. Still, as the foregoing observations have clearly shown, though not at all so fully as I might have shown, the great disadvantage our country labours under, in having no effective court of inquiry in cases of death under suspicious or mysterious circumstances; and as through this defect many culprits escape justice, and much indirect encouragement is given to crime—it behoves us, as watchful guardians of the health and lives of our fellow-countrymen, to lift up our united voices against the continuance of such a state of matters, and to call upon the legislature to remedy the defects of which we complain. Dr Granville of London, in a letter addressed to me on the subject of the coroner, advises the appointment of a barrister as coroner, assisted by a medical superintendent, a physician of long standing, and not in practice, whose special duty it would be to make a *post-mortem* examination, and to examine witnesses on all questions concerning the health, treatment, and cause of death, of the deceased. This is most obviously a good suggestion for the improvement of the English coroner's court; but inasmuch as we have no such court in Scotland, it does not apply to us.

Several methods, as applicable to Scotland, might be suggested. The plan pursued in our East Indian Possessions, of invariably having a medical adviser, is most excellent, and merits consideration. Another method has been suggested, viz., making it imperative, that in all cases of sudden death, or death under suspicious or extraordinary circumstances, if any legally qualified medical practitioner shall refuse to certify, in writing, the cause of death, on the ground that he considers it to have been attended with circumstances demanding investigation, it shall be the registrar's duty immediately to transmit that refusal to the procurator-fiscal, and call upon him to investigate the cause of death before it is inserted in the register. One of the requisites of the registry ought to be to show *the cause of death.* The attending expense should be defrayed by the crown. The chief objection to both of these plans is, that a medical man may be required to advise and give a certificate in the case of his own patient; which, for obvious reasons, as I have shown, is sometime not desirable, to say the least of it.

As far as the prosecution of a case, after evidence has been obtained, is concerned, the practice in Scotland, if effectively carried out, seems to be unexceptionable;[1] but in doubtful cases, the law authorities very rarely sanction a *post mortem* examination, and yet seem to expect medical men to give an opinion—the data for which they are prevented from obtaining, and that apparently for no other reason than an ill-judged parsimony. I regard a certificate as to the cause of death, obtained from a mere external inspection, or "view" of the body, in the vast majority, if not in all cases, as utterly worthless, except as simply to testify the fact of death; yet such certificates are asked for by the legal authorities, and, I understand, sometimes even granted by medical men.

As the most obvious method of improving this state of matters, however impracticable at the first blush it may appear, I would suggest for serious consideration, the appointment, under government, of certain qualified medical practitioners, not in practice, to particular districts; the registrar to report every case of death to such medical inspector, under a penalty. It should be his duty, in all cases of sudden death, or death under suspicious or extraordinary circumstances, or even from preventable causes, to make a careful examination into every particular, directly or indirectly bearing upon

[1] Dr Lonsdale of Carlisle, while giving credit to the "*crowner's quest law,*" in clearing up many unaccountable deaths, which, in Scotland, would escape "the precognition," yet admits, that the sheriff sifts everything to the bottom, *when a case is taken up,* and holds up Scotland as an example to England in in that respect. Lawyers tell us that the Scotch practice is superior in every respect to that of England,—if so, why is it not acted upon, and effectively carried out? But the want of the medical element in both countries is an evil requiring remedy.

www.ingramcontent.com/pod-product-compliance
Lightning Source LLC
LaVergne TN
LVHW052028160826
845678LV00003B/1240

* 9 7 8 0 3 5 3 4 5 8 9 9 4 *